Fraser Island Travel and Tourism

Vacation, Tour, a Guide

Author
David Mills.

SONITTEC PUBLISHING. All rights reserved. No part of this publication may be reproduced, distributed, or transmitted in any form or by any means, including photocopying, recording, or other electronic or mechanical methods, without the prior written permission of the publisher, except in the case of brief quotations embodied in critical reviews and certain other noncommercial uses permitted by copyright law. For permission requests, write to the publisher, addressed "Attention: Permissions Coordinator," at the address below.

Copyright © 2019 Sonittec Publishing
All Rights Reserved

First Printed: 2019.

Publisher:
SONITTEC LTD
College House, 2nd
Floor
17 King Edwards
Road,
Ruislip
London
HA4 7AE.

Table of Content

SUMMARY 1
INTRODUCTION 4
FRASER ISLAND 9
   FRASER ISLAND HISTORY 9
   FAST GUIDE 12
   TRAVEL HOLIDAYS TOURISM 34
   FRASER ISLAND ACCOMMODATION - HOLIDAY ACCOMMODATION 37
      Accommodation specials for Fraser Island 41
   FRASER ISLAND ACTIVITIES & ATTRACTIONS 43
   FRASER ISLAND HOLIDAY WITH KIDS 51
   FRASER ISLAND BARGE SERVICE 54
   FRASER ISLAND BEAUTY SPOTS 56
   FRASER ISLAND CAMPING 60
   FRASER ISLAND CRUISES 62
   FRASER ISLAND 4WD RENTALS 64
   FRASER ISLAND RESORTS 66
      Eurong Beach Resort - 3 Star +, Beachfront Resort - Fraser Island 67
      Mercure Kingfisher Bay Resort - Accor - 4 Star Eco Resort 76
   FRASER ISLAND TOURS 92
   FRASER ISLAND WHALE WATCHING 95
   TOP ATTRACTIONS OF FRASER ISLAND 97

Summary

The world is a book and those who do not travel read only one page.

It is indeed very unfortunate that some people feel traveling is a sheer waste of time, energy and money. Some also find traveling an extremely boring activity. Nevertheless, a good majority of people across the world prefer traveling, rather than staying inside the confined spaces of their homes. They love to explore new places, meet new people, and see things that they would not find in their homelands. It is this very popular attitude that has made tourism, one of the most profitable, commercial sectors in the world.

People travel for various reasons. Some travel for work, others for fun, and some for finding mental peace. Though every person may have his/her own reason to go on a journey, it is essential to note that traveling, in itself, has some inherent advantages. For one, for some days getting away from everyday routine is a pleasant change. It not only refreshes one's body, but also mind and soul. Traveling to a distant place and doing exciting things that are not thought of otherwise, can rejuvenate a person, who then returns home, ready to take on new and more difficult challenges in life and work. It makes a person forget his worries, problems, frustrations, and fears, albeit for some time. It gives him a chance to think wisely and constructively. Traveling also helps to heal; it can mend a broken heart.

For many people, traveling is a way to attain knowledge, and perhaps, a quest to find answers to their questions. For this, many people prefer to go to faraway and isolated places. For believers, it is a search for God and to gain higher knowledge; for others, it is a search for inner peace. They might or might not find what they are looking for, but such an experience certainly enriches their lives

Introduction

If you are ever looking for an island holiday destination in Australia, the coast of Queensland is the go-to place. It is endowed with one of the most diverse array of islands you'll ever find anywhere, ranging from sand to continental to coral cay islands.

Little wonder the islands and resorts located on the Great Barrier Reef have become the most sought after.

The Queensland coast boasts multiple coral cays that are home to world-famous island resorts which include, among others, the Green Island

Resort (5-star), Heron Island Resort (4-star), and the Lady Elliot Island Resort (3-star). This magnificent trio offers wide-ranging experiences when it comes to accommodation styles.

That aside, another top attraction that continues to draw holidaymakers here is the unmatched snorkelling or diving experience, where it's even possible to walk in straight off the beach.

We are in the Home of Fraser Island
In 1972 UNESCO adopted the World Heritage Convention to protect special places for all humanity. Fraser Island was World Heritage listed by UNESCO in 1992 in recognition of its natural values.

The official citation pays tribute to the island's "exceptional natural beauty" and refers to "over 250km of sandy beaches with long, uninterrupted sweeps of ocean beach, with more than 40km of strikingly coloured sand cliffs, as well as spectacular dune blowouts and ocean surf beaches; tall rainforests growing on low nutrient sands; perched dune lakes including both clear "white water" lakes and dark "black water" lakes; banksia woodlands, heath, patterned swampy fens and sheltered mangrove areas in a spectacular "mosaic landscape."

Fraser Island provides a globally significant example of geological processes and biological evolution, including: complex coastal dune formations that are still evolving; an array of lakes that is exceptional in terms of number, diversity, age and the evidence of dynamic and developmental stages; and outstanding examples of ecosystems that have developed in response to maritime conditions and poor soils in coastal dune formations.

The whole of the island is part of Great Sandy National Park (other than freehold areas such as townships) and is protected under the Nature Conservation Act 1992 and the Recreation Areas Management Act 2006 to the low water mark.

That aside, another top attraction that continues to draw holidaymakers here is the unmatched snorkelling or diving experience, where it's even possible to walk in straight off the beach.

The local Butchulla people call it K'Gari paradise and for good reason. Sculpted from wind, sand and surf, the striking blue freshwater lakes, crystalline creeks, giant dunes and lush rainforests of this gigantic sandbar form an enigmatic island paradise unlike anywhere else. Fraser Island is the largest sand island in the world (measuring 120km by 15km), and is the only known place where rainforest grows on sand.

Inland, the vegetation varies from dense tropical rainforest and wild heath to wetlands and wallum scrub, with sandblows, mineral streams and freshwater lakes opening onto long sandy beaches. The island, most of which is protected as part of the Great Sandy National Park, is home to a profusion of bird life and wildlife, including the famous dingo, while offshore waters teem with dugong, dolphins, manta rays, sharks and migrating humpback whales.

Fraser Island

Fraser Island History

The history of Fraser Island began with the Butchulla people who were the original aboriginal inhabitants of the region. They called it K'gari which can be translated to mean "paradise". There was a sizeable population of aboriginal people on Fraser Island due to the abundance of food and fresh water. The aboriginal people occupied the Fraser Island region for at least 5000 years prior to the first Europeans coming on the scene. Matthew Flinders sailed this section of Australia's east coast in 1802 and called into Fraser Island to replenish water supplies and fire wood. Botanical specimens were also collected for return to be studied in England.

In 1836 the "Stirling Castle" was wrecked on Fraser Island and the survivors lived with the aborigines until rescued by a search party from Brisbane. Eliza Fraser was one of the passengers and after the death of her husband from natural causes, toured the world telling of the hardships she endured. The island was originally named Fraser's Island by European settlers after Eliza Fraser.

In more modern times Fraser Island has been a source of wealth from mining, timber and tourism. There were considerable deposits of rutile on Fraser Island and the sands were mined for this resource from 1949 until the 1970's when the islands tourism potential and a protest campaign brought this activity to an end. Fraser island was also logged very heavily as the forests there contained many valuable species. The Satinay in particular was heavily logged. It is the world's hardest hardwood and impervious to marine worms. The shores of the Suez Canal were lined with its timber, removed from the forests of Fraser Island. Inevitably, the practice of logging on Fraser Island was terminated and the forests left to regenerate and today very little evidence of these practices can be seen.

In 1992 Fraser Island was added to the world heritage list and is now protected by this and National Park status. It is now one of Australia's leading tourist attractions and its pristine lakes and magnificent rainforests attract thousands of tourists every year. Fraser Island is best reached from Hervey bay or Rainbow Beach and you can fly direct to Hervey Bay from Sydney or Brisbane. There are also resorts with four star or three star accommodation on the island. Kingfisher Bay resort is the most popular of these.

The history of Fraser Island may be troubled but the majesty of all of its natural attractions are now preserved for all time.

Fast Guide

Fraser Island is the largest sand island in the world, world heritage listed and stretching over 100km along the southern coast of Queensland. A place of exceptional beauty, with long uninterrupted white beaches flanked by strikingly coloured sand cliffs. The island has over 100 freshwater lakes, some tea-coloured and others clear and blue all ringed by white sandy beaches. Ancient rainforests grow in sand along the banks of fast-flowing, crystal-clear creeks.

Fraser Island is a precious part of Australia's natural and cultural heritage, it is protected for all to appreciate and enjoy.

Fraser Island is the only place in the world where tall rainforests are found growing on sand dunes at elevations of over 200 metres. The low "wallum" heaths on the island are of particular evolutionary and ecological significance, and provide magnificent wildflower displays in spring and summer.

The immense sand blows and cliffs of coloured sands are part of the longest and most complete age sequence of coastal dune systems in the world and they are still evolving. They are a continuous record of climatic and sea level changes over the last 700 000 years. The highest dunes on the island reach up to 240 metres above sea level. The Great Sandy Strait, separating Fraser Island from the mainland, is listed by the Convention on Wetlands of International Importance (Ramsar Convention). The wetlands include: rare patterned ferns; mangrove colonies; sea-grass beds; and up to 40,000 migratory shorebirds. Rare, vulnerable or endangered species include dugongs, turtles, Illidge's ant-blue butterflies and eastern curlews.

Climate:

At 500km south of the Tropic of Capricorn, Fraser Island has a hot and humid climate but is cooled by sea breezes. Its summer maximum average temperature is only 30 degrees C, although the summer months have some extremely hot days. Winters are mild, with average temperatures of around 15 degrees C. This is usually the dry season and most winter days are sunny and frost free, making for a very pleasant climate. People with fair skins need to be wary when out in the midday sunshine since unprotected skin can burn in a few minutes. Hats, cool clothing that protects from the sun, sunscreen and common sense are essentials to enjoying Fraser Island summers.

Getting there

By boat: Vehicular access to Fraser Island is by ferry only; thereafter, four-wheel drive vehicles are necessary for transport around the island. Travelers have the option of bringing or hiring their own 4WD vehicle, joining a group from a Hervey Bay hostel, or taking a 4WD tour bus. Vehicle hire is available and tour buses depart from various towns on the Sunshine Coast (Noosa) and Fraser Coast (Hervey Bay).

The following boats serve Fraser Island:

Fraser Venture (Ph. +61 7 4125-4444) - vehicle barge that makes three crossings per day from River Heads (10km southwest of Hervey Bay) to

Wanggoolba Creek (west of Central Station / Eurong).

<u>Fraser Island Ferry Service</u> - crosses from Inskip point near Rainbow beach to the southern point of Fraser Island. Most trips originating from Noosa use this service.

<u>By air</u>: A number of charter operators fly light aircraft on to Fraser Island, landing on the main beach (at low tide only).

<u>Fees and permits</u>: Permits - Vehicles and Camping: All vehicles travelling to Fraser Island must have a permit. It must be attached to the windscreen. Campers other than those using commercial camp sites must have a camping permit which should be attached to the tent in clear view for inspection by the park ranger.

Permits are available from the following offices:

- The Department of Environment Smart Service Qld www.qld.gov.au/camping 13 13 04
- Brisbane: 160 Ann St, +61 7 3227-8185
- Maryborough: Cnr Alice and Lennox St +61 7 4121-1800
- Gympie: +61 7 5482-4189
- Noosa: +61 7 5447-3243
- Bundaberg: +61 7 4153-8620
- Rainbow Beach: +61 7 5486-3160

Permits are also available from:

- The Marina Kiosk Buccaneer Avenue
- Urangan Boat Harbour +61 7 4128-9800
- National Parks Kiosk River Heads boat ramp

Get around
By car: One of the most enjoyable ways to visit Fraser Island is by 4WD. To visit most of the main sites, you should allow three days. You can hire

vehicles with camping gear or stay in accommodation on the island.

- Fraser Magic 4WD Hire, +61 7 4125-6612. Family run business, with a Swiss-Australian background. Provides 4wd hire from 2 up to 8 seater landrovers. Accommodation or camping packages available (updated Aug 2017
- Fraser Island Tagalong Tours. Fraser Island Tagalong 4WD Tours for the budget traveler. (updated Aug 2017 | edit)
- Nomads, e-mail: bookings@nomadsnoosa.com. 4wd tag-along tours on Fraser Island. Three days' tours with a guide (fully equipped with sat phone and first aid kit, new Fraser Island regulations for 4wd companies). (updated Aug 2017
- Atlas4wdhire provide well maintained 4wd vechicles and great service. +61 419 886006

Driving can be quite difficult especially during the dry season as the sand roads can be very difficult to get through. The sand can become like talcum powder and it is not uncommon if a vehicle becomes stuck to have to wait for hours before a bus can come by to tow the car out. The best time to drive is after there has been some rain when the sand road is more solid. Getting stuck relies on the help of others to get out. If you are not comfortable driving, taking a tour is recommended. Typically the longer the tour is, the smaller the group travelling.

Seeing

Lake MacKenzie - the jewel of Fraser Island, Lake MacKenzie is a large perched lake with crystal blue waters and white sands. The area is one of the most popular on the island so can get crowded during the middle of the day in peak season. There are toilet facilities and an enclosed picnic area - no food or drink is to be consumed outside of this area in an attempt not to attract dingoes.

<u>Lake Wabby</u> - a green colored barrage lake approximately 45 minutes walk from the beach, with a large sand blow that is slowly encroaching upon the lake. Freshwater turtles and catfish can sometimes be seen swimming in the lake. The path to the lake will split with only 100m difference between the two however the slightly longer way takes you over a sand dune. This split is well marked. If you take the one way into the lake over the sand dune you will be walking down the sand dune - much easier than up the sand dune.

On the way out, walk along the lake with the lake on your right and you will see the second path at the edge of the lake taking you through the rainforest. Walking through the sand dune can get quite hot during the summer and it's a good idea to bring water along. Locals bring bodyboards to slide off the sand dune into the lake. Do not run into the lake off the sand and attempt to dive. Many people get seriously hurt and even paralyzed trying to do this every year. The only toilet facilities available are at the beginning of the walk in.

Indian Head - the rocky outcrop at the northern end of the main beach. Climb to the top to look down into the ocean and spot sharks, rays, turtles and dolphins. Beautiful outlook.

Champagne Pools - north of Indian Heads, these rock pools provide a safe place to bathe in sea water. Their name is derived from the froth created when waves break over the edge and into the pools.

Eli Creek - a freshwater creek midway along the main beach where bathers can float or walk down with the slow current. The water in the creek can vary quickly but does not get above waist height of an adult 5'9". The deeper parts can usually be avoided by walking on the other side of the creek. A boardwalk provides access to the top of the creek. It is an easy walk both on the boardwalk and through the water.

<u>1 Maheno shipwreck</u>. The SS Maheno had been a passenger steamer, travelling between New Zealand and Australia and used by the NZ Navy as a hospital ship during World War one. The Maheno was retired and, in 1935, the SS *Maheno* was being towed to Japan for scrapping when a cyclone off the coast forced it ashore. The wreck of the Maheno sits a few km north of Eli Creek.

Doing
One of the best ways to see Fraser Island is to hire a 4WD and explore at your leisure. Accommodation options range from basic cabins

to 4 star resorts. Another popular option is camping on the beach or at inland campgrounds - most vehicle hire companies also hire camping gear. If time permits you should allow at least three days to discover the wonderful sights of Fraser. To ensure quality of service it is recommended to hire from a company that is a current member of the Fraser Coast 4X4 Hire Association.

Get wet and go wild

There are so many different ways to get wet on Fraser Island. No visit to the island is complete without a long leisurely float in the beautiful blue waters of Lake McKenzie, a perched lake fed only by rainwater, encircled by pure white sand. Lake Wabby, at the edge of the Hammerstone Sand Blow, is the deepest lake on the island and when the sun shines it's hard to resist plunging into its cool, emerald depths. Eli Creek is a clear freshwater creek — you can walk along its boardwalk then float with the current all the way to the beach. Champagne Pools, where the surf crashes over a series of rock walls into a calm but bubbly rock pool below the headland on the northern tip of the island, is another top spot to cool off. See them all on a self-guided 4WD adventure, or join a Beauty Spots Tour, which also includes the rainforest.

Step out on the Fraser Island Great Walk
The Fraser Island Great Walk is a 90 kilometre (56 mile) track that winds between Dilli Village and Happy Valley, passing most of the island's notable sites, such as Lake McKenzie, Wanggoolba Creek, Lake Wabby and the towering rainforest trees in the Valley of the Giants. To do the whole thing takes about six days — make sure to book campsites along the way — but if that sounds a bit

too energetic there are plenty of short walks you can do for a half day or as an overnight adventure.

Drive the beach

All roads on Fraser Island, which are made of soft sand, are 4WD only. A number of tours are available, or you can hire your own set of wheels on the island or in Hervey Bay. If you haven't driven on sand before, the friendly folk at Aussie Trax 4WD Hire at Kingfisher Village will give you a quick lesson before you set out. Most people head straight to the vast sandy highway otherwise known as 75 Mile Beach on the eastern side of the island, but also worth doing is the inland Central Lakes scenic drive (allow about two hours), highlights of which include Pile Valley's impressive stand of tall, straight satinay trees, Lake McKenzie, and Lake Wabby lookout for a view of Lake Wabby and Stonetool Sand Blow.

Shine a light on the local wildlife

Wild nightlife takes on a whole new meaning on Fraser Island, where many of the natives come out to play once the sun goes down. Join a ranger on a guided night-time walk, shining a spotlight on the trees and into the bushes to see sugar gliders leaping through the treetops, rare frogs at the lake edges and other wild animals as they rustle through the scrub. At just AUD$5 it's a bargain-priced night's entertainment.

Camp on the beach or stay in style at Kingfisher Bay Resort

Fraser Island has accommodation to suit every budget. There are eight campgrounds – you can hire camping equipment when you hire your 4WD – and if you really want to get back to nature you can camp behind the dunes on Eastern or Western Beach. Kingfisher Bay Resort has a four-star hotel, self-contained villas and beach houses. If you're backpacking, accommodation is all part of the deal when you join a Cool Dingo Tour.

<u>Get mugged by a whale</u>
Ever wondered where whales go on their holidays? Each year thousands of whales migrate from the cold Antarctic waters to the warmer tropical seas along Australia's east coast to give birth, and on the way back many stop to rest in the sheltered waters of Hervey Bay before returning south. Between August and late October this is one of the best places in the country to see humpbacks with their calves as sightings are almost guaranteed. If you're really lucky you might even be on a boat that gets "mugged" by the whales when they come right in close. Half day whale watch cruises cost AUD$120 and operate August 1 to October 31.

Eating
While you will need to be relatively self sufficient for food if you aren't staying at on of the resorts,

the resorts do have restaurants attached and are open to visitors. This said, Eurong Beach Resort has a bakery which sells pies, sausage rolls and some sweet treats as well as fresh baked bread. The shops at Eurong, Happy Valley, Cathedrals on Fraser and Orchid beach have *basic* supplies.

<u>1 Seabelle Restaurant</u>, Mercure Kingfisher Bay Resort, +61 7 4120 3333. Fresh Australian seafood and bushtucker, drawing inspiration from the indigenous Butchulla tribe from the island. (updated Jul 2018

Drinking

Soft drinks and alcohol can be purchased from shops at Eurong and Happy Valley, although alcohol is not available before 10AM due to state licensing laws. Note that prices are substantially higher on the island than on the mainland; save money by bringing sufficient supplies with you!

Drinking water can be obtained from taps in various campsites and from a tap on the beach 500m north of Eurong; untreated water from the creeks or lakes should not be drunk.

Sleeping

The prow of the wreck of the *Maheno* juts above the sand.

Sleeping on Fraser Island ranges from luxury resorts through campsites to rough camping amongst the dunes along designated stretches of beach.

Lodging: 1 Eurong Beach Resort, +61 7 4127-9122. With rooms to suit a variety of budgets, Eurong sits towards the south of the main beach on the east side of the island. Many guests will join 4WD bus tours offered by Australian Sunset Safaris from the resort. The area also contains shops, fuel and other facilities, though note that prices are substantially greater than on the mainland. From $140.

Kingfisher Bay Resort and Village, +61 7 4120-3333. A more upmarket option on the west of the island, but it also has some cheaper huts, with restaurants, pubs and shops. It's possible to stay here in isolation. Not many daytrippers pass by, and its a little remote from the 4wd beaches, etc.

Sailfish on Fraser, +61 7 4124-0287. Beautiful appointed 2 bedroom apartments at cosy Happy Valley.

Waiuta Retreat, +61 419722098. Hoilday house at Kingfisher Bay Resort. Private, quite location adjacent the National Park with great views. (updated Dec 2017

Camping

There are a number of camp sites on the island which house standard facilities (toilets, showers etc.) and are fenced to keep dingoes out. Fires are permitted in these sites within fire rings, but noise is forbidden after 9PM. Never bring any food inside the tents as dingoes will tear apart the tents looking for it - even if it's already gone they can still smell the food that was there and will look for it. When possible keep food in a dingo cage off of the ground. There is also a camp ground at Central Station and this must be pre-booked.

Backcountry: Along the main beach, there are designated areas for camping amongst the dunes. These are marked by wooden signs indicating areas where camping is permitted and where it is forbidden. In all cases, a permit is required to camp, and in some areas advanced bookings are required.

During busy periods, arrive early in the day to ensure your camping area. Camp fires outside of the official campsites are no longer permitted, with Rangers patrolling the beach and issuing fines for infringements. Be dingo safe; lock all food away when unattended.

Stay safe

Fraser Island is home to approximately 150 dingoes - Australia's wild dog. These animals can become aggressive - a 9 year old boy was killed in 2001 - and should not be approached or fed. Feeding of dingoes carries a $250 fine, and all food should be secured (in vehicles or food boxes) when unattended.

Swimming in the ocean is not recommended owing to both the dangerous surf conditions and the number of sharks that inhabit the waters (Indian Head is a shark breeding ground).

Drive safely on the sand and obey the speed limits - the beach is classed as a highway, so police will run speed checks and breath tests for drivers. Speed limit on the main beach is 80km/h and on soft sand tracks 30km/h, unless otherwise signed.

Due to the temperate climate, saltwater crocodiles are not normally present within Fraser Island's waterways. However, there have been reports of crocodiles sighted in the Fraser Coast region, including on Fraser Island. This is *very* rare and almost unheard of, yet the presence of a large (4 meter) male saltwater crocodile was reported in March of 2009. The crocodile, however, was not captured so the report remains inconclusive.

David Mills

Travel Holidays Tourism

For the inquisitive traveller, who wants to know everything they can do and see on Fraser Island, this is the place to be. Fraser Island is well documented as the world's largest sand island and one of Australia's most important world heritage wilderness areas. It is also one of the countries best known family holiday destinations for those who love the great outdoors and a magnet for international travellers, especially those who are following the backpacker trail. Anyone can easily get to Fraser Island. Coaches and trains run regular services to nearby mainland destinations and airline services fly direct from Sydney and Brisbane to Hervey Bay.

Fraser Island is a unique destination for many reasons. Firstly, there are no roads and you must hire a four wheel drive vehicle to get around or travel on one of the many organised tours or camping holidays. Accommodation is available in either resort style, holiday homes and apartments or backpacker lodges. Access to and from the island is via a vehicular ferry which runs from River Heads to the east coast of Fraser Island or from Inskip Point to the islands southern tip. Light aircraft provide aerial scenic flights and access to the ocean side of the island where they land on the beach.

Any visitor to Fraser Island is in for a scenic treat. The island is famous for its magnificent stands of pristine rainforest that have withstood the rigours of a past logging industry and a history of sand mining. Its large number of perched and window lakes are amazing and its ocean beach is almost endless. Some of its best loved natural attractions include Lake Mackenzie with its white silica sand beaches, Wangoolba creek, Eli Creek, The Maheno shipwreck and the Cathederal coloured sand cliffs. At the northern end, Indian Head and the Champaign Pools are frequently visited. Fraser Island is also a National Park containing a wide variety of native flora and fauna. It is the home of the huge Satinay tree which provides the world's hardest hardwood. So hard it was actually used to line the banks of the Suez Canal when it was built.

The population of Fraser Island Dingoes that remain here are the most pure of the Dingo breed still in existence.

Fraser Island has a history including a long relationship with Australia's indigenous Aborigines who called it K'Gari which means paradise. In early European times, a number of shipwrecks occurred, one of which gave the island its name when a woman by the name of Eliza Fraser became an unwilling resident of the island and lived for several years with the local Aboriginals before being rescued. Everything taken into account, Fraser Island is one of Australia's best and most interesting places to visit.

Fraser Island Accommodation - Holiday Accommodation

Fraser Island accommodation suits the needs of all holidaymakers. There is a wide range of holiday homes in a number of locations on the island as well as caravan park style cabins, self contained holiday units together with backpacker< and four star hotel accommodation. Accommodation on Fraser Island is located on the Great Sandy Straits side where Mercure Kingfisher Bay Resort is located as well as on the ocean side in townships like Eurong beach, Cathedral beach, Happy Valley and Orchid Beach. The accommodation on Fraser Island can be accessed from either Hervey Bay by vehicular ferry or fast catamaran which runs a regular service to Kingfisher Bay Resort. Car ferries operate from both Inskip Point in the south, River heads and from Hervey Bay itself.

Kingfisher Bay Resort is the leading resort on the island and they have accommodation ranging from hotel rooms through to fully self contained 1, 2 and 3 bedroom apartments. The three bedroom banksia executive units and the two bedroom

Pandanus units feature multilevel pole house type construction and are located on the hill behind and overlooking the resort. These units feature spas and top quality inclusions. The hotel suites are roomy and located close to the pools and restaurants that are a feature of this wonderful resort. There are three swimming pools and three restaurants of different standards and the main resort building is an architectural masterpiece as it blends into the ecological surroundings of the Fraser Island forest and lakes. Kingfisher Bay resort also offers a wide range of Fraser Island tours to visit the islands many beauty spots.

Eurong Beach resort is situated on the ocean side of the island. This resort caters more to the budget and middle range in the market. The resort caters through fully self contained units through hotel style suites and most are located close to the magnificent swimming pool. There is also a large new restaurant and a small shopping centre which includes a bakery and convenience store. The resort is situated right on the ocean beach and is the jumping off point for many of the islands tours. Four wheel drivers will find Eurong to be an excellent central point from which to explore many of Fraser Island's magnificent beauty spots.

As you travel north along the beach from Eurong you will first come to Happy Valley. Here you will find both Sailfish on Fraser and Fraser Island Backpackers. Sailfish consists of 10 modern two bedroom apartments with all modern facilities. There is a swimming pool as well as undercover parking. Fraser Island Wilderness retreat is nearby and this property features self contained cabins of excellent standard together with a swimming pool, restaurant and convenience store. Frasers at Cathedral Beach is a popular destination featuring self contained holiday cabins, convenience store, liquor and fuel facilities as well as camping areas with shower and toilet facilities. Scattered along the ocean front there are numerous holiday homes available. These are very popular and must be booked well in advance. They are mostly located at Orchid Beach in the north, Happy Valley and Eurong Beach.

The Fraser Island region is totally unique in Australia.

Accommodation specials for Fraser Island

Welcome to our Fraser Island Specials website! Every traveller is looking for holiday deals and in Australia this website is the best place to find them. You will find special offers and bargain buys on a wide range of products including the best choice of places to stay from a variety of providers including Hotels, Motels, Resorts and Holiday

Apartments, as well as a number of Fraser Island tour packages and day trips.

Fraser Island product range is very wide spread with plenty of information on all types of holiday products including on tours, auto rentals, camper vans and motor homes, yacht and boat charters. There are also a large number of specials and packages to help you plan your next holiday at the best possible price. Fraser Island has a great quantity of natural beauty, a rich history and a vast array of activities and sightseeing.

This website is designed to deliver deals, specials and packages, be sure to bookmark this website and check back regularly as we will be frequently adding new offers. Fraser Island specials, bargains and offers are snatched up very quickly so if you see something you like – grab it before you miss out!

Fraser Island Activities & Attractions

Fraser Island's breathtaking natural environment and spectacular position on the Great Barrier Reef makes it the ideal holiday destination for those wanted to relax and get back to nature or get their heart pumping with a bit of adventure on the world's largest sand island. However you choose to spend your time on the island, Fraser has a wonderful range of activities and attractions to suit everyone.

Fraser Island's experiences are many and varied including majestic whale watching off Hervey Bay during the annual migration season, beautiful Lady Elliot Island and the wonder of the World Heritage listed Great Barrier Reef as well as the rare rainforests that grow on the island, the unique sand dunes, pristine beaches and crystal waters, expansive 144km coastline, MAHENO shipwreck and the wide variety of plant life and native wildlife species.

Fraser Island is also renowned as a four wheel driving hot spot, with most of the island accessible by 4WD. Seventy Five Mile Beach is actually a highway that runs along the surf side of the island and the sand tracks that link the lakes and rainforests on the island are a great way to see the amazing scenery of Fraser. However please note, vehicle access permits are required for all vehicles entering the island, otherwise visitors are able to hire 4WD's on the island.

Seventy Five Mile Beach is also right in the heart of the action for some of the world's best beach fishing. Surf gutters occur naturally off the beaches providing excellent angling conditions and no matter when you choose to visit, you'll always be able to catch something with bream and whiting aplenty during the warmer months and swallowtails available year round. Rock species are caught off the Waddy Point to Indian Head headlands while trailer boats are available for launching into the calm waters. For southern reef and northern coral species, off shore is your best bet.

Enjoying such a picturesque and naturally blessed location, Fraser Island's leisure pursuits all revolve around exploring or enjoying its dazzling and unique environment and ecosystems.

Central Station: Offers a delightful boardwalk along Wanggoolba Creek, visit the peaceful Basin Lake, or stand among some impressive satinay trees in Pile Valley.

Lake McKenzie: This inland perched lake is a very popular site with white sand and pristine sparkling blue water, in summer the visitor numbers are restricted.

Lake Boomanjin: This is the largest perched lake in the world, covering almost 200ha. Its waters are stained brown by tannins leached from the vegetation.

Lake Wabby: This is the deepest lake on Fraser Island and is a deep green in colour and is surrounded by forest on one side and the advancing edge of the Hammerstone Sandblow on the other, a truly magnificent site and well worth the walk in.

Eli Creek: Cool off in the crystal clear waters of Eli Creek or take the boardwalk to the top of the creek and float down with the flow to the beach. Eli Creek pours up to four million litres of fresh water into the ocean every hour.

Kingfisher Bay Resort: Is located on the western side of the island is a worth a visit if you need to pick up a few supplies, there is a small supermarket and bakery that serves a good coffee.

Champagne Pools: Are located just north of Indian Head and rock pools filled with salt water and an ideal spot to cool off at low tide.

Wungul Sandblow: Enjoy expansive coastline views from the first dune crest of this sandblow.

Wreck of the S.S. Maheno: Originally built in Scotland in 1905 the S.S. Maheno was a luxury passenger ship. In 1935 the ship was considered outdated. While being towed from Melbourne to Japan it encountered a cyclone and drifted on to 75 Mile Beach on Fraser Island. The ship is now severely rusted and climbing is not permitted.

75 Mile Beach: Many of these attractions are located along 75 Mile Beach. The Beach runs along

most of the east coast of Fraser Island. While not the best place for a swim due to dangerous currents it abounds in beautiful landscapes and a varied wildlife. Due to the nature of the hard sand the beach acts as a highway and a runway.

Lake Allom: Tucked into a rainforest hollow, this lake offers a cool respite from the beach environment. A circuit track around the lake meanders through a variety of plant communities. Wait on the viewing platform and watch for freshwater turtles, but please do not feed them.

Waddy Point Headland: Take in a vista of beach and ocean. Watch for sea turtles, sharks and stingrays coasting along.

Binngih Sandblow (Waddy Point): Catch sweeping views across Waddy Point headland and north over Marloo Bay to Sandy Cape, the site of the only lighthouse on Fraser Island.

Ocean Lake: Ocean Lake is home to a variety of water birds taking advantage of the reeds and undisturbed sections of the lake. Nearby, an easy walk through cypress, banksia and melaleuca woodland offers a good lookout with panoramic views.

Holiday activities on Fraser Island will keep your family entertained for days. If you are booking into Fraser Island accommodation, you will find that there are plenty of activities close by to keep the whole family amused.

Four-wheel driving is the order of the day on Fraser Island as there are no made roads and the kids will love to go exploring the lakes and rainforests or drive along the ocean beach.

Fishing is one of Fraser Island's most popular activities. The beaches are usually the best and the deep gutters and rips can produce a multitude of different species. Dart and flathead are common. Around the Indian Head region large catches of tailor are common and many other species as well. The annual fishing classic on Fraser Island is one of its major attractions and tens of thousands of visitors every year. It is a catch and release event to make sure that fish stocks in the region remain strong. First prize is usually a four wheel drive vehicle.

Organised tours are another great activity that you and your family can do. Either from Rainbow Beach in the south or from Hervey Bay in the north, you can join a tour that will take you to experience all of the islands beauty spots.

On the ocean beach you will visit Eli Creek, where you can swim in crystal clear fresh water then visit the wreak of the old Maheno whose rusting structure still defies the elements as she slowly decomposes. The coloured sands are just a little further north. Inland you will see pristine lakes and visit age old rainforests with magnificent stands of tall trees.

One of the most popular holiday activities on Fraser Island is camping, and tens of thousands of campers visit the island every year. Some are family groups with their own equipment while others are backpackers who hire a vehicle and camping gear from suppliers in Hervey Bay or Rainbow Beach. They all have a great time and go home singing the praises of the fabulous specials, activities and attractions on Fraser Island.

Fraser Island Holiday with Kids

Fraser Island is the best place to take the kids for a holiday. All children love to go camping and fishing or playing beach sports and maybe exploring fascinating lakes and rainforests. Fraser Island is filled with these activities and much more so your kids will be entertained for as long as you want to stay. Local island accommodation isavailable in resorts of different standards, self contained apartments or in holiday homes, most of which are only walking distance to the beach. Your other option which is also very popular is to take the kids camping on the island. At the time of writing this you are able to camp anywhere you like on Fraser Island. There are however, moves afoot to restrict camping to dedicated camping areas. These are currently available at Central Station, Eurong, Happy Valley, Cathederal Beach, Dundaburra or at Orchid beach.

Fraser Island is a kids paradise. Except for the odd hungry dingo there is little danger and the dingos and other Fraser island wildlife, must be treated with respect. There is so much for the kids to see and do. Visiting the beauty spots, swimming at Lake MacKenzie is a fantastic experience with its blinding white sand and crystal clear waters, it is the ideal place to stay for a couple of days. The ocean beach is miles long and is ideal for surf fishing and beachcombing. The stands of rainforest on Fraser Island are unique in the world in that it is the only place known where rainforests grow in sand. The Yidney Scrub rainforest and Central Station and Woongoolba creek regions are supremely beautiful. The kids will also enjoy visiting the Maheno ship wreak, the coloured sands, Indian Head and the champagne pools.

If you choose to take the kids to a resort, there are two main ones to consider. Mercure Kingfisher Bay resort is a four star resort located on the western side of the island and has lots of kids activities. Eurong Beach resort is a three star resort and is located on the ocean beach and often has holiday specials. Fraser Island can be accessed by barge from Hervey Bay in the North or from Rainbow Beach in the south. You can take your own four wheel drive vehicle to Fraser Island on the barge.

Fraser Island is one of Australia's best family holiday destinations and the kids will love it.

Fraser Island Barge Service

The great majority of people visiting Fraser Island arrive on the barge service. Apart from chartering a light plane, there is no other way to access the island from the mainland. There was a fast catamaran service to Mercure Kingfisher Bay resort on the islands western side but this has now been terminated. The barge service gives you the opportunity to also transport your four wheel drive vehicle to the island. There are a number of options as to where you can depart the mainland and where you can land on Fraser Island.

At the islands southern end, most people drive along the beach from Rainbow Beach to Inskip Point. From here there are two barges that run continuous services back and forth across the channel. They both carry passengers, tour buses and private four wheel drive vehicles. The barges commence operations at 7 am and continue services until around 5 pm. Generally speaking, the crossing is not affected by weather except in extreme circumstances.

If you want to access Fraser Island from the Hervey Bay end there are two options that you can choose from. The Fraser Dawn barge operates from the Urangan Boat Harbour, both morning and afternoon and takes vehicles to the Moon Point landing at the southern end of the western beach. Barges also operate regular services from River Heads about twenty minutes drive south of Hervey Bay. One service will take you to Kingfisher Bay resort and this service takes both walk on passengers and vehicles. The other service from River Heads gives access to the Woongoolba Creek ramp from which you can access the ocean beach and the attractions in the center of the island like Lake MacKenzie and Central Station.

The cheapest barge service to Fraser Island is the one via Inskip Point.

Fraser Island Beauty Spots

The beauty spots on Fraser Island and the history will take your breath away. Some of the things you will see when you visit Fraser Island, although different from the things you will see in other parts of the world, will astound you with their natural beauty. Fraser Island is famous for many things but the thing you will cherish most are the memories of its magnificent lakes and rainforests and the clarity of the beautiful streams. Fraser Island is very easy to get to. You can fly direct to Hervey Bay from Sydney or Melbourne or you can bring your own four wheel drive vehicle and bring it across on the barge from either Rainbow Beach or Hervey Bay. If you are not self driving you can join one of the organised tours that run daily to the island. These tours can take you for one, two or three days and the extended ones are accommodated on the Island.

The places that you must visit while visiting Fraser Island include.

- Central Station. This region is the main camping and administration area for the rangers who control the island. Here you will find Woongoolba Creek which is one of the islands major waterways. It is crystal clear and winds through the local rainforests. A boardwalk has been built parallel to its banks to protect the local ecosystems. The rainforest here are quite spectacular and you can follow the boardwalk all the way to Pile valley where you will see giant Satinay trees. It was from this region that these trees were logged to provide the wall linings of the Suez canal.

- <u>Lake McKenzie</u>. This lake is the most photographed icon on Fraser Island. It consists of the clearest fresh water you will ever see surrounded by beaches of pure white silica sand and windswept paperbark trees bent into magnificent shapes.

- <u>Eli Creek</u>. This is the largest fresh water creek on the ocean beach side of the island. It pours tens of thousands of litres of the purest fresh water into the ocean each day. It is surrounded by a boardwalk and is one of Fraser Islands most popular swimming places.

- The <u>Maheno Shipwreck</u> and the Coloured Sands. The Maheno was wrecked on the ocean beach in the thirties. It has been used as a target for bombing practice during the war years yet it still presents an impressive sight for tourists travelling along the beach. The coloured sands are located nearby and here you will find beautiful sand cliffs with a myriad different colours.
- <u>Indian Head</u> and the Champagne Pools. Indian head is the only rock area on Fraser island. All the rest of it is sand. The headland provides a fantastic vantage point to overlook the ocean and from here you will often see turtle and sharks swimming below. The champagne Pools are a fantastic place for a swim as the waves continually wash more water into the pools as you swim.

> There are many other places to go however these are the most commonly visited beauty spots on Fraser Island.

Fraser Island Camping

Camping on Fraser Island is one of life's great pleasures. There are very few world heritage wilderness areas left on the planet where campers are welcomed and there are excellent facilities to cater for them. Fraser Island has everything a camper dreams of. There is fantastic scenery, plenty of fresh water, easy access and a safe environment. There are so many people who enjoy camping on Fraser Island and thousands of them return every year for their annual holidays. At the time of writing this there is no restrictions on where you can camp on the island. There is however, debate in the media about restricting camping to dedicated camping areas. The debate about feeding dingos or not feeding dingos goes on and many people feel that if campers are restricted to properly controlled camping areas the dingo problem will be reduced.

Fraser Island is famous for its wildlife and fishing and tens of thousands of beach fishing aficionados have come to Fraser Island to try their luck. The annual fishing competition sees thousands of fishermen and their families camped at Orchid beach at the northern end of the island to try their luck at catching a special fish that will win them the annual prize of a brand new four wheel drive vehicle. Many families with kids love to come to Fraser Island to camp on the beachfront for the annual school holidays. There are so many places of interest to take the kids that are superbly beautiful.

Lake Wabby, Lake Birrabeen, Lake Mackenzie and many others each have their own charm and resident wildlife. The tropical rainforests are magnificent with tall forest of Satinay and Kauri Pines covering an understory of ferns and vines. Both Central Station and the Yidney Scrub Rainforest areas are a must to take the family. Camping gives you so many options of places to stay and the cost of your holiday is kept to a minimum. Fraser island can be reached by road from Hervey Bay or Rainbow Beach and then barges are available to carry you and your four wheel drive to the island. If you want to go camping on your next holiday, then come and see Fraser Island.

Fraser Island Cruises

There are lots of Fraser Island cruises and tours which mostly depart from Hervey Bay. The fast catamaran service to Mercure Kingfisher Bay resort on Fraser Island has been discontinues from March 2010 and access is now provided via the vehicular ferry from River Heads. Another vehicular ferry operates from Hervey Bay to Moon Point and this is probably the most convenient one to take if you are taking your own vehicle to the island for a holiday. Whale watching tours will also pick up from Kingfisher bay rsort on fraser island as part of the morning tour aboard the Quick Cat Tour. Outside of the Whale season, the Tasman Venture Two operates cruises to the northern end of Fraser Island. And customers will see the sandy cape lighthouse and the Woothumba creek region which can be explored on kayaks.

Fraser Island Cruises will take you to see this fantastic world heritage listed wilderness area.

Fraser Island 4WD Rentals

Aussie Trax 4X4 Rentals

We at Aussie Trax offer self-drive 4WD's for touring the largest sand island in the world, the magnificent World Heritage Listed Fraser Island.

Drive 90 mile beach, camp in the dunes under the stars by your camp fire, see the dingoes and the amazing bird life, take a walk in the rainforest, take a swim in one of the many freshwater lakes which vary in colour from brown through to green and blue or see the sharks and rays from Indian Head to name a few.

We have been part of this for the past 10 years and are by far the longest-established operators and we also have the widest range of vehicles. A Fraser Island 4WD Adventure is a must do for the adventurous at heart whilst travelling the east coast of Australia and driving yourself is the only way to guarantee you see all the best places on Fraser Island at your own pace.

We comprehensively brief all hirers on all aspects of their trip and supply them with maps and itineraries that can suit anyone's plans. We can also organise accommodation on the island or supply you with a camping package if you wish.

Camping Equipment Supplied:
Tent, roll mats, ice-box, torch, water container, gas cooker, utensils, pots, plates, axe, shovel, groundsheet.

Available on request: table, chairs, gas light, sleeping bags - extra cost applies
Free pick-up and drop off in Hervey Bay.

Aussie Trax 4WD Hire - From Kingfisher Bay
Aussie Trax 4WD Hire provides modern, well equipped 4 wheel drive vehicles for hire from Kingfisher Bay Resort. You have the choice of a

Toyota Land Cruisers that seat seven passengers or a Suzuki Jimny that seats two passengers.

4WD rental from Kingfisher Bay Resort is a fantastic option for independent families who wish to explore Fraser Island in their own time, on their own agenda, but with plenty of expert help from Aussie Trax staff before they leave!

Fraser Island Resorts

Fraser Island resorts and hotels are some of the most popular places to stay for international tourists. The Island has three resorts of different standards, two of which are on the ocean side and one is on the inshore side. Mercure Kingfisher Bay Resortis the highest standard and is a four star eco resort with international accreditation. It overlooks the waters of the Great Sandy Straits which separate Fraser Island from the mainland. The resort has over two hundred rooms, three restaurants, several swimming pools and is accessed by a direct barge service from River Heads on the mainland. The best Island resorts also has other options like Eurong beach resort on the ocean Beach. This is a three star resort and has a shopping center as well. Happy Valley, Cathederal Beach and Orchid Beach also have accommodation of one form or another.

Beautiful Fraser Island, world famous as being the largest sand island, with fabulous beaches & forestry is an ideal holiday destination.

Eurong Beach Resort - 3 Star +, Beachfront Resort - Fraser Island

Property Information:
Eurong Beach Resort's absolute beachfront position gives easy access to the vast expanse of Fraser Island's famous Seventy-Five Mile Beach.

It is also centrally placed to visit the southern lakes, which include McKenzie and Wabby, as well as the rainforests around Pile Valley and Central Station.

General Facilities

- Two swimming pools
- Restaurant
- Two Bars
- Reception (7am - 8pm)
- Cafe
- Bakery
- General Store
- Petrol Station
- EFTPOS
- Major credit cards accepted (some surcharges may apply)
- Guest laundry fully equipped
- Tennis

- ➢ BBQ
- ➢ Fishing gear hire
- ➢ Joy Flights
- ➢ 4WD Tours
- ➢ Disabled facilities

Restaurant

Eurong Beach Resort is located right on the Fraser Island ocean beach. There are many hectares of tropical gardens.

A major refurbishment in the late 1990s saw a huge new swimming pool and a number of new accommodation units added to the resort.

The fun place to be is the casual Beach Bar which has entertainment most nights. Relax with a drink under the palms trees overlooking the beach or swim in the pool.

Shops

Eurong is a most popular place on the island to shop for supplies with fuel, bakery and a convenience store.

A bakery supplies fresh bread and pastries, pizza, casual snacks, coffee, drinks and ice cream.

Accommodation Information:
Accommodation is designed to suit all budgets and ranges from motel units to two-bedroom apartments.

Spacious self-contained motel units have double or twin beds and day beds, which make two single beds for children. Units have a decks or patios, fully-equiped kitchenettes, showers and toilets.

Self-contained, two-bedroom apartments

accommodate up to six people and have large living areas, decks, fully-equipped kitchens, bathrooms and balconies.

Location Information:

How to Get There

Barges: Fraser Island Barges have several services daily from River Heads, south of Hervey Bay and Rainbow Beach.

Ex River Heads 20 mins south of Hervey Bay:: 50 mins to Kingfisher Bay Jetty =
09:00, 12:30, 15:30, 18:45
Per Vehicle (1-4 pax) one way $95
Per Vehicle (1-4 pax) return $160
Extra passenger one way $6
Extra passenger returns $12

Ex Rainbow Beach / Inskip Point: The 30-minute crossing operates on demand and during daylight hours.

Fly / Drive

By Air to Fraser: Air Fraser operate scenic flights and air transfers ex Hervey Bay and ex Sunshine Coast, to Fraser Island daily. A range of packages are available including your scenic flight, accommodation and 4WD vehicle hire.

By Air to Hervey Bay - Fraser Coast: Virgin Blue operate direct flights from Sydney with connecting flights from other ports. Qantas Link operates direct flights from Brisbane.

By Rail to Hervey Bay: Tilt Train from Brisbane or Rockhampton to Maryborough with QR Rail-link bus to Hervey Bay.

By Coach to Hervey Bay: A scheduled coach transfer service departs daily from Brisbane. Greyhound and Premier operate daily from Brisbane and Cairns.

Things to Do

Tours: Leave the driving to someone else and take a day or
2 day Fraser Explorer Tour and see all the major

sites including Lake McKenzie and Indian Head with an expert local guide.

Tours operate daily from Hervey Bay and Rainbow Beach and include: courtesy pickup from your accommodation, all meals and multi-share accommodation (upgrades available to motel & apartments), for two day tours.

Click on the links below to get itineraries and more details.

Don't just imagine... join a Fraser Explorer Tour and discover the best of this World Heritage wonder!

4wd Packages: Eurong Beach resort is only accessible by 4WD vehicle. If you don't have a 4WD and would like to have the freedom to discover Fraser on your own, take a 2 or 3 day 4WD Hire Package.

Fraser Island

Fishing: Fishing enthusiasts from around the world come to Fraser Island to experience one of Australia's most rich and diverse fishing areas. The fishing is some of the best in the world and available on your doorstep at Eurong Beach Resort.

Fishers are required to observe size and bag limits and are urged to take only what they need in order to protect the fish resource.

Beach fishing is popular at Eurong Beach Resort where surf gutters along the ocean beaches provide all-season angling.

Whiting and bream are plentiful in these gutters in warmer months and swallowtail can be caught all year round. The tailor season in winter sees dozens of fishing camps along the beach.

Tides & Permits

Tides: Driving on Fraser Island's Seventy-Five Mile Beach is subject to tides and the general rule is to make sure you are off the beach for two hours either side of the high tide.

Permits: Vehicle access permits are required for all vehicles entering the island. Camping Permits are also required in advance for camping. Permits may be obtained from River Heads Barge Office, at Kingfisher Bay Resort reception and at Queensland National Paks and Wildlife Service offices including Brisbane, Hervey Bay, Maryborough, Bundaberg and Rainbow Beach.

4WD Driving Conditions: Speed limits are 80km/h on the beach highways and either 35km/h or 20km/h on the inland tracks. Drivers need to be responsible and make themselves aware of the conditions before setting out.

Emergency: There is a Police Station at Eurong. First aid and emergency medical assistance can be obtained from the Queensland Parks and Wildlife Service ranger stations. In the event of an emergency please call 000.

Mercure Kingfisher Bay Resort - Accor - 4 Star Eco Resort

Property Information:
Mercure Kingfisher Bay Resort is located on beautiful World Heritage listed Fraser Island, the resort is eco-friendly as the whole resort has been designed within it's surrounding rainforest. Kingfisher Bay Resort is a fantastic place to stay while exploring the island, either with a guided tour or bring your own 4WD with you to Fraser Island and explore this untamed wilderness with it's hundred's of tracks, ancient rainforests, coloured sand cliffs and the Seventy-Five Mile

Beach. Fraser Island is the world's largest sand island.

Mercure Kingfisher Bay Resort's accommodation varies from resort rooms for couples to fully self contained eco villas for large families. The resort features swimming pools, restaurants & bars, gift shop & general store, tennis, water sports, guided island tours and offers conference, events & wedding facilities.

Facilities:

Four swimming pools	Four bars
Three restaurants	Conference facilities
Cafe	General store
Gift shop	Post office and stamps
Spa Sanctuary	Austec Playground
Child minding	Porter service
24 hour reception	Major credit cards accepted (surcharges may apply)

EFTPOS	Disabled facilities
Spa	Tennis
Safety deposit boxes	Water sports
Guest laundry and dry cleaning service	
WIFI in hotel rooms	

Conferences, Events & Weddings:

Kingfisher Bay Resort has an experienced Conference Management Team that can organise any activity to suit your particular agenda whether it's an elegant dinner in the wilderness, a four-wheel-drive safari or a challenging outdoor adventure-based training program with low rope courses and team games. The resort offers unique outdoor venues with quality service, facilities and equipment.

The resort has a Wedding Manager to organise you special day, from a simple ceremony at romantic

Sunset Beach to a ceremony in one of the many peaceful bush settings around the resort.

Cocktail parties, barbecues and elegant or formal dinners can also be arrange. They can be held in a spacious air-conditioned ballroom, or in a more casual environment like the deck overlooking the pool or beachside.

Accommodation Information:

Resort Hotel Room
Enjoy the best of the bush from the private native-timber deck, brew a coffee in-room and indulge in the moment, or soak up the smells and sounds of the land as you wander their timber walkways. And when the day is done, stretch out in air-conditioned comfort on the Queen or King-single beds and reflect on a day well-spent.

Up the ante on your eco-experience with a room

upgrade to a sea view, spa room and wake to sunshine glinting on the waters of the Great Sandy Strait.

The hotel room features include air-conditioning, TV, phones, private balcony, tea/coffee facilities, ironing equipment and hair dryer.

Ask about their interconnecting, spa rooms or facilities for guests with special needs.

Villas

2 Bedroom Villas:

Enjoy the time with family and friends in the resort's Villa-style hideaways, nestled discreetly in the treetops. After a lazy day visiting lakes and lagoons, you can slip into your own spa bath as the sun goes down, or escape to your own private corner of the villa with a book and a smile.

Enjoy bush or sea views from your private deck and for ultimate indulgence upgrade to a villa with spa on the deck.

All their two bedroom villas have:

Fully equipped kitchen, laundry, colour TV, telephone, bath/showers and ironing equipment.

3 Bedroom Villas:
Keep your eyes peeled as daylight fades on another Fraser day, as local wildlife comes out to play, or guess, what colour the sunset will be from the comfort of your deck. Enjoy a home-made breakfast with the birds from your own private veranda whilst planning the day's adventure.

Then it's just a short hop to the Resort Village Shop for provisions, the Centre Complex for a Ranger Guided Walk or Ranger's desk just for a yarn.

All their three bedroom villas have:

Fully equipped kitchen, laundry, colour TV, telephone, bath/showers and ironing equipment.

Location Information:

Getting to The Island

Self Drive

From Brisbane

The journey is approximately 3.5 to 4 hours drive north of Brisbane City. Head out of Brisbane city on the Inner City Bypass onto Kingsford Smith Drive. Stay on Kingsford Smith Drive until you see the signs to the Airport on the Gateway Arterial Road. Once on the Gateway Arterial Road, you continue driving for around 10 minutes until you see a sign that says 'Sunshine Coast' on the left lanes.

Take this exit and drive for a further 10 minutes until this joins the Bruce Highway. You then simply follow the signs through Gympie then take the Maryborough exit. From Maryborough, it is about a 20 minute drive when you reach a big round about, turn right here and follow the signs towards the Hervey Bay Airport. Before reaching the airport there will be a right hand turn (with a big Fraser

Island/River Heads sign), turn here and drive towards the River Heads Shopping Village where you will see the Kingfisher Bay reception area.

From Bundaberg

The journey is approximately 1.5 hours drive south. Follow the Bruce Highway south to the Fraser Coast. Turn off at Torbanlea and follow signs, at the end of this road you will come to a big round about, go straight through to Hervey Bay Airport. Probably a 10-15 minute drive you see on the right a big River Heads/Fraser Island sign, turn right and keep driving till you reach the River Heads Shopping Village where Kingfisher bay reception is located.

Kingfisher Ferry Service:

Kingfisher Ferry has 4 services to the resort each day from River Heads. This ferry has seating for 220 passengers on two decks with a fully licensed bar and snack food available. The journey takes approximately 50 minutes.

Kingfisher Bus Transfer Service

Mercure Kingfisher Bay Resort will provide regular scheduled pick up / drop off guest courtesy transfer services between key locations such as Hervey Bay Coach Terminal and Urangan Harbour to River Heads to meet the ferry departures - for all passengers including walk-ons. These transfers must be pre-confirmed at time of booking.

2013-2015 AIRPORT TRANSFERS	
HB Airport to Kingfisher Mainland Reception	
	Adult-Child-Infant
One Way	$18.00
Return	$20.00

All rates are in Australian Dollars and are valid from 1 April 2013 till 31 March 2015

2013-2015 FERRY TRANSFERS		
	Adult	Child
One Way	$25.00	$12.50
Return	$50.00	$25.00

All rates are in Australian Dollars and are valid from 1 April 2013 till 31 March 2015

KINGFISHER FERRY TIMETABLE				
	Departure Times			
Departs River Heads (Hervey Bay)	9:00	12:30	15:30	18:45
Departs Mercure Kingfisher Bay Resort Jetty	7:50	10:30	14:00	17:00

Please note: Operating only on Friday and Saturday. There are no Mainland Porter services to transfer guests to carpark facilities or for bus transfers to Hervey Bay available off the 2300 ferry departure.

Secure Parking

Secur parking is located at River Heads. Check-in at Kingfisher Bay Resort Terminal at the River Heads shopping village.

Self Drive with 4wd Drive

Barge transfers at River Heads with your 4WD vehicle:

River Heads is about 15 minutes north of Maryborough. Follow the signs to Hervey Bay and mid-way through the journey, you will see a sign for 'RIVER HEADS'. Turn right at this sign onto Booral Road, then travel for approximately 10 minutes until you will see a sign for 'RIVER HEADS Fraser Island Barges'. Turn right at the sign onto River Heads Road. From there, it is about a 10 minute drive straight to the ferry terminal. You should aim to collect your barge tickets at least 20 minutes prior to your departure.

Barge transfers at Inskip Point, Rainbow Beach with your 4WD vehicle:

Turn off the Bruce Highway at Gympie onto the Tin Can Bay Road; continue following all Rainbow Beach signs to township (approximately 60 minutes traveling). From Rainbow Beach follow Inskip Point Road to its end – where you will see the white barges.

2013-2015 BARGES TRANSFERS	
	Per Vehicle
Ex - River Heads	$160.00 return (vehicle & 4 passengers)

All rates are in Australian Dollars and are valid from 1 April 2013 till 31 March 2015

BARGES TIMETABLE
Fraser Island Barges runs daily services to Wanggoolba Creek and Mercure Kingfisher Bay Resort from River Heads. The journey is approximately 30 minutes.

River Heads to Kingfisher Bay Jetty	Departure Times			
Departs River Heads	9:00	12:30	15:30	18:45
Departs Kingfisher Jetty	7:50	10:30	14:00	17:00

All transfers time are subject to changes without advance notice. Please check with reservationss at the time of booking for the current schedule.

Island Activities & Tours

With the ability to choose to either explore Fraser Island or relax in the comfort of Mercure Kingfisher Bay Resort in style you really are in for a one fun holiday. Sip a cocktail by one of the four swimming pools, play tennis, bubble in a spa, indulge in a massage, enjoy good food and wine or just go fishing and get the chef to cook your catch. The kids will have fun with the Eco Ranger program or at the Kid's Club.

The resort plays host to many natural attractions like magnificent rainforests, beautiful fresh water lakes, mighty sand dunes, a spectacular Seventy-Five Mile Beach, Shipwrecks, abundant wild life.

You can discover Fraser Island with a ranger to guide you on our 4WD coach tours or personalised safaris. Guided nature walks range from bird watching to spotlighting for the creatures of the night. Cruise the calm island waters to find dolphins, dugong and turtles and, from August to October, humpback whales.

ACTIVITIES:

Tennis	Volleyball, Beach cricket
Sailing lessons	Three swimming pools
Dinghies, canoes & paddle skis	Free guided nature walks
Sailing catamarans & sailboards	Island slide shows
Pool tables & gaming machines	Junior Eco Rangers

| Aussie Trax 4WD Hire | |

Tours:

TOURS		
TOUR TYPE	TOUR DESCRIPTION	2014/15 RATES
Beauty Spot 4WD Tour	This Beauty Spots 4WD Tour departs from Kingfisher Bay Resort, and you'll visit the top natural attractions, cool off in watering holes, sit in an air-conditioned comfortable, custom-designed four-wheel-drive coach. HIGHLIGHTS Gorgeous Lake McKenzie Central Station and Wanggoolba Creek Pile Valley's stunning Satinay and Brush Box forests Seventy-Five Mile Beach's famous highway The Maheno shipwreck and the	Adult: $160 Child: $110 (4-14yrs)

	coloured sands of The Pinnacles		
	The temperate, fresh waters of Eli Creek		
	The mighty Stonetool Sand Blow		
	Available: Daily.		
CRUISES			
CRUISE TYPE	CRUISE DESCRIPTION	2014 RATES	
Whale Watching	Quick Cat II is equipped with a hydrophone, allowing guests to listen to the live underwater sounds of the male humpback composers and an underwater viewing camera, which beams images onto screens around the boat. You'll also enjoy expert commentary; home-made morning tea provided; Children's activity booklet; Wheel chair and pram access; Advanced Ecotourism accreditation; whale information available in English, French, Italian, Spanish, German, Chinese, Japanese and Korean. Available: August to October.	Adult: $110 Child: $70 (4-14yrs)	

All rates are in Australian Dollars and are valid from 1 April 2013 till 31 March 2015

Fraser Island Tours

Tours on Fraser Island are positively the best way to see the island. There are a number of tour companies available and tours can be sourced from Hervey Bay, or. You can take your pick from self drive camping tours through one day tours, two day camping or accommodated tours or three day camping or accommodated tours. Some are designed to appeal to the backpacker market whilst others are more suitable for families. There are also exclusive tours for those who like less numbers, better meals and higher standards of Fraser Island accommodation. Also available is a multitude of four wheel drive hire options including fly drive packages. Whale watching trips are also available from Kingfisher Bay Resort.

The Fraser Explorer Tours offers a unique range of tours from and are very experienced. Their tours include a one day tour, a one day exclusive tour, a two day accommodated tour and a three day camping adventure. Kingfisher Bay resort and offer a huge range of tours from Hervey Bay, Rainbow Beach and Noosa. They have both a one day tour and an exclusive tour. They are also the only company whose tour includes Lake Mackenzie. They also have a two day accommodated tour. Many of the backpacker hostels in Hervey bay have self drive camping tours at very reasonable rates. operate from Brisbane and have some excellent accommodated 2 & 3 day tours as well as a day tour. During the season, Kingfisher Bay resort offers tours from the resort to Platypus Bay on the inshore side of Fraser Island to view the magnificent humpback whales. These creatures migrate through the area and tours are available from mid July through to early November.

There is also the option of hiring your own four wheel drive and camping gear and just setting off on your own. Hervey Bay is a great jumping off point for this type of activity with regular vehicular barge services available to the island from Urangan Boat harbour or River Heads and these will deliver you to Moon Point, Kingfisher Bay Resort or Wangoolba creek on the Fraser Island side.

Australian Travel Wholesalers have been specializing in booking Fraser Island for over 15 years and our staff knows the island inside out. Don't hesitate to call one of our staff for help or advice. Our freecall number from within Australia is 1800 815 378 or from overseas +61 7 4128 6607. You can also email us for help. When Fraser Island tours are available as specials or packages they are displayed on our specials website

Fraser Island Whale Watching

Fraser Island is a great place for shore based **whale watching**. Every year between the months of May and July and then again from September to November pods of migrating Humpback whales travel along the coast as part of their annual migration. They can be spotted every day as they come close to the coast. The best places to go whale watching from along the ocean shoreline of Fraser Island are the higher points of land like Indian Head which is the easternmost point of the island. The height of the headland gives the whale watcher a great view as the animal's pass by. It is also common to spot large turtles, dolphin and sharks in the shore break here.

On the northern and north eastern side of the island Fraser Island borders the Marine Park where the Hervey Bay whale watching vessels go to show their customers the Humpback whales. The ocean swells here are broken by Fraser Island and this provides a calm water bay where the whales come to have their calves and suckle them prior to their arduous migration back to Antarctic waters. The whales here have become used to the boats and it is common now for them to swim right up to the boats and investigate the whale watchers.

Mercure Kingfisher Bay resort, which provides the best resort style accommodation on Fraser Island, lies on the western side of Fraser Island runs whale watching trips into the marine park on one of their fast catamarans. The Fraser Island and Hervey Bay regions are the best place in the world to go whale watching and the industry here is now 25 years old so the operators are really experienced and recognize many of the whales that return year after year.

If you want to go whale watching or take the kids whale watching, there is no better place than Fraser Island

Top Attractions of Fraser Island

The largest sand island on the planet, World Heritage-listed Fraser Island is one of Australia's most rewarding four-wheel-drive adventures. Most of the 123 km-long island, which lies off Australia's east coast between Bundaberg and Brisbane, belongs to Great Sandy National Park, a protected area of diverse habitats and dazzling beauty. Subtropical rainforest, seemingly endless beaches, mangroves, lagoons, towering sand dunes, and crystal clear freshwater lakes are just some of the features nature lovers can explore.

Once home to the Butchulla indigenous people, Fraser Island was formed over many millions of years as sediment eroded from the Great Dividing Range. Prevailing southeasterly trade winds and rivers swept the sand to the sea, dumping it in dunes up to 250 m high. Today, visitors can see the evidence of an island still evolving: in the shifting sand dunes, the sea-sculpted shores, and rain and wind-lashed coastal cliffs.

The spirit of adventure is palpable on this windswept island. Miles of dune-backed beaches rim the coast, creating a sandy highway for self-drive visitors and tour vehicles. Stories of rental vehicles swept away in rising seas are a somber warning for drivers to heed the tides. But for many visitors, this merely adds to the excitement.

Exploring Fraser Island
Scenic drives are a great way to see more of the island in less time, but drivers should note that the

island lacks any sealed roads; 4WD vehicles are essential. Furthermore, the soft sand tracks in the island's interior require high-clearance 4WD vehicles with low range capacity.

Another rewarding way to explore the island is on foot. Hiking trails thread through the wilderness, providing an up-close perspective on the island's diverse flora and fauna. A particularly challenging, but beautiful hike is the 90 km **Fraser Island Great Walk,** which takes in some of the island's top attractions. Mountain bikers can ride along the eastern beach, however the soft sand elsewhere on the island should be avoided.

Besides off-road driving, hiking, and biking, top things to do on the island include fishing off the eastern beach, swimming, birding, mountain biking, and camping. For those not planning on pitching a tent, the limited accommodation options for tourists range from the well-known Kingfisher Bay Resort on the island's west coast, to apartments, and a small beach resort.

Although tour companies offer day trips to the island, a visit of at least two to three days is recommended to appreciate the contrasting features and cover the island's main attractions.

75 Mile Beach
Driving along the sweeping wave-thrashed shore of 75 Mile Beach is a fitting introduction to one of the most unique 4WD safaris in the world. Skirting the east coast of Fraser Island, the road is a National Highway and also serves as a landing strip for light aircraft. Along its roughly 120 km stretch, visitors can see the rusted hull of the Maheno shipwreck; the multicolored cliffs of the Cathedrals; and the bubbly rock pools, called Champagne Pools. Look for the occasional shark fin slicing through the sea - a warning to unsuspecting

swimmers that tiger sharks prowl these waters. Dangerous surf and strong riptides are a further deterrent for those seeking a relaxing dip.

Maheno Shipwreck

About 10 km north of the tiny settlement of Happy Valley, the Maheno shipwreck, once a trans-Tasman liner, is a popular attraction along 75 Mile Beach. In 1935, a cyclone swept the boat ashore while it was being towed from Sydney to Osaka. The eight crew on board camped on the beach for a couple of days until help arrived, but the ship could not be refloated and attempts to sell the vessel were unsuccessful. Today, its rusted skeleton is a haunting landmark along this wind-whipped stretch of coast.

Plants

Fraser Island's fascinating plant life has adapted to thrive in its sandy soils. Along the coast, salt-tolerant plants such as beach spinifex and purple trumpet flowers anchor the dunes. In the subtropical rainforest near Central Station, tall brushbox, giant kauri, and hoop pine dominate. Ferns, strangler figs, climbing vines, and orchids add texture and color. This area is also home to the impressive king fern, which grows and sprouts the largest fronds in the world.

In the island's interior, smooth-barked forest red gums and scribbly gums grow in the tall eucalypt forests. Also found here are bloodwoods, string-barked satinays, and much-coveted blackbutts, which were the mainstay of the thriving timber industry.

Wildlife
Fraser Island's rich variety of fauna reflects its diverse habitats. On land, visitors may spot: dingoes, reputedly Australia's purest strain; sugar gliders; brushtail possums; flying foxes; snakes; and sand monitors among others. Birding is also

superb. More than 354 species have been spotted on the island, including pied oystercatchers, white-bellied sea-eagles, brahminy kites, yellow-tailed black-cockatoos, and king-parrots. Off the coast, there are humpback whales, dolphins, dugongs, stingrays, turtles, and sharks (particularly tiger sharks). After strong winds and wild seas, blue bottles with long stingers sometimes wash ashore.

Lakes
Fraser Island is dotted with more than 200 freshwater lakes and creeks, some of which are perfect for a refreshing swim. The lakes are a fascinating reflection of the geology, and three different types are found on the island: perched, window, and barrage lakes. Perched lakes are filled solely by rainwater. An impermeable layer at the base of the lake prevents the water from draining completely through the soil. Window lakes form in low-lying areas when the ground level dips below

the water table, while barrage lakes occur when large sandblows or shifting dunes, trap the water from natural springs.

One of Fraser's most-visited attractions, stunning Lake McKenzie (Boorangoora), offers a striking combination of sublime white sand and cool, clear waters in vivid shades of blue. The sand here is actually silky-soft silica, which filters the rainwater of this perched lake, making it so pure that it supports little aquatic life. Many visitors come here to sprawl on the satiny shores and swan about in the crystal clear water. Lake McKenzie is also a popular camping spot. On the eastern side of the island, Lake Boomanjin is the world's largest perched lake. Tannins leached from the vegetation impart a brownish color to the water.

Lake Wabby is both a window lake and Fraser's only barrage lake. The towering Hammerstone

Sandblow bordering its blue-green waters is engulfing the lake by about a meter per year, a testament to the constantly evolving landscape. This is Fraser's deepest lake and the only one to support a few varieties of fish. It's also a sacred men's site to the Butchulla tribe. From here, Lake Wabby Track leads to a lookout with superb views of the wind-sculpted landscape and the water it is quickly smothering.

Central Station
Once the center of logging operations, Central Station now displays exhibits on island history and ecology, and marks the starting point of some picturesque hikes. Wanggoolba Creek, with its crystal clear waters weaves through subtropical rainforest here, and a boardwalk follows the fern-fringed creek through picabeen palms, vines, and strangler figs. Hikers can continue on a trail

through forests of tall eucalypts to the shores of beautiful Basin Lake.

Eli Creek
Eli Creek is a popular picnic and swimming spot along 75 Mile Beach. Deceptively powerful, the creek pours about 4 million liters of fresh water into the sea every hour. A pandanus-fringed boardwalk along the creek leads to a bridge where children like to splash about and float down its fast-flowing waters. Keep an eye out for jungle perch, eels, and frogs. Drivers should take care when crossing the creek in a vehicle as it often carves deep channels along the beach.

The Cathedrals
On 75 Mile Beach, about 18 km south of Indian Head, the island's most easterly point, the Cathedrals are multi-colored sandstone formations sculpted by the wind and rain. Red, yellow, and orange hues predominate thanks to iron oxides in

the sand. The Cathedrals provide a great photo opportunity - especially in the soft glow of dawn.

Fraser Island Great Walk
The 90 km Fraser Island Great Walk traces the tracks of old logging routes and the island's first human inhabitants, the Butchulla people. The trail passes some of Fraser's most popular tourist attractions such as crystal-clear Lake McKenzie, the subtropical rainforest and historic exhibits of Central Station, Wanggoolba Creek, and dune-backed Lake Wabby. The trail runs between the settlements of Dilli Village and Happy Valley.

Visit Lake McKenzie
My favourite place on Fraser Island and one of the most beautiful places I've seen has to be Lake McKenzie. This huge, freshwater lake is perfectly clear and reflects the bright blue sky above, making it seem magical and almost unbelievable. It's the perfect place to stop for a swim and the

amazing thing about it is, the water is so clear you can see everything. It makes for an unforgettable experience.

Drive the 75 Mile Beach 'highway'
Yep, it's a highway that's also a beach. It comes with road signs, police speed cameras and everything! Load up your 4WD and drive along this iconic beach highway that is, yep you guessed it, 75 miles long. It's also a very popular spot for beach fishing and during peak season, you'll find hundreds of keen fishermen and women lined up

3. Float down Eli Creek

Eli Creek is another favourite spot of mine and a place I can't wait to visit again. Walk the boardwalk through the bush until you reach the end, then jump in the fresh, cool water and let it carry you along the gently winding path down toward the ocean. It's incredibly fun and beautiful and a must-do when visiting Fraser Island. Bring a tube or floaty device for bonus points!

Catch a fish or two

Fraser Island is a haven for people who love to go fishing. The island swells with keen fishermen and women hoping to bag Whiting, Dart, Bream, Mackerel, Tailor, Trevally, Tuna and Flathead. Popular fishing spots to throw in a line include Indian Head, Middle Rocks, Sandy Cape and Waddy Point.

Visit the Maheno Shipwreck

There's a good chance you may have seen photos of the shipwreck before as it's frequently photographed and easily recognisable. The wreck was bound for a Japanese wrecking yard when she came to her demise during a cyclone, washing ashore in 1935. Now, she's rusty and majestic and a must-visit on Fraser Island.

Take a scenic flight

Hop on board a GA8 Air Van with Air Fraser Island, you'll take off and land on the beach and see some absolutely amazing things during your flight. Get a birds-eye view of the island most beautiful spots and keep your eyes peeled for marine life!

Spot Humpback Whales
If you visit between August and November, keep your eyes peeled for these gentle giants. The whales are on their migration during this period, seeking out the warmer waters in preparation for calving. Bring your binoculars and keep your eyes peeled for a puff of water on the horizon, spraying from their blowholes.

See Central Station and Wanggoolba Creek
Central Station was once a forestry camp and was established when there was still logging on Fraser Island. This area is now surrounded by gorgeous rainforest and a fantastic boardwalk that takes you past the clear, flowing waters of Wanggoolba

creek. It's an easy way to explore a section of the rainforest, see some huge trees and absolutely stunning stag-horns nestling in among them.

Play cricket on the beach
Pack your own cricket set, set up our stumps and have a good old fashioned game of beach cricket! You could also pack a footy, soccer ball or frisbee too. Just be sure to be sun smart out there in the harsh Queensland sun.

Visit the Stonetool Sand Blow
Take in the sheer size of the Stonetool Sand Blow. It's an active blow which covered the forest but is slowly uncovering it as the sand moves across the island.

Stand on the world's largest sand island
Ahhh, yep, that's what Fraser Island is! It is the world's largest sand island and is heritage listed too, which is pretty impressive when you think

about it. It's literally all sand, stretching over 120km, it's huge!

Forage for bush tucker
If you visit or stay at Kingfisher Bay Resort on the island, they run a few different tours that are fantastic. A really good one to take is a tour that teaches you about bush tucker and how to forage for food out in the bush. It's a great way to learn a newfound respect for what's around you and how the Indigenous communities survived off the land.

Eat a fancy meal at the Seabelle Restaurant
While you're there, stop in for dinner at Kingfisher Bay Resort's Seabelle Restaurant. The food here is really delicious, taking its inspiration from the Indigenous Butchella tribe. The menu combines seasonal, local produce with fresh seafood and Australian bush tucker to create a modern, delicious and unique menu well worth sampling.

Be Dingo safe

Fraser Island is the unique home to a dingo population. There are dingo attacks each year but, as the locals will tell you, most are avoidable. It's important you're aware of the dingo presence and take steps to be safe, including not doing anything bone-headed like trying to take a dingo selfie or feeding them your food. They aren't domestic dogs, they're wild animals and it's important to respect that.

Watch the sunset
The sunsets on Fraser Island are absolutely stunning and you should take in as many of them as possible. A great place to watch them is from the beach in front of Kingfisher Bay Resort. You get to see the sun go down on the horizon, setting the sky ablaze with bright orange, red, yellow and pink light.

Watch the sunrise

It's no surprise that the sunrise here is pretty special too, so get yourself out of bed before first light, wrap a blanket around your shoulders and watch the day come alive. It's a memorable experience.

Have a BBQ
I'm not one to point fingers, but you pretty much can't call yourself an Australian or a visitor to Australia unless you have a BBQ near the beach. It's mandatory. If you don't do it, our government will kick you out and make you wear the cone of shame. You'll need a BBQ, an esky full of potato salad, regular salad, meat, seafood, buns, lots of sauce and lots of beer.

. Sit on the jetty at Kingfisher Bay Resort
Head down to the Kingfisher Bay Resort jetty and pull up a seat for an incredible sunset. It's also a fantastic place for fishing and also for great

photographs too. Just be aware it's not kosher to take beers/alcohol in general down there.

See the coloured sands
If you find yourself at Eli Creek, take the short trip up to the coloured sands, which are made up of some 72 different colours. The colours are caused by the leaching of oxides, which coat each grain of sand and create different colours, mostly tones of red and yellow.

Visit Lake Wabby
Visit Lake Wabby while you can, because over the next century or so it will be lost due to a sand dune moving westward across Fraser Island. This window lake was created when the ground level fell below the water table and formed a deep green pool of water.

Sandy Cape Lighthouse
Take a trip to the heritage-listed Sandy Cape Lighthouse on the most northern point of Fraser

Island. It is the tallest lighthouse in Queensland, built in 1870 ad is one of only two lighthouses in Australia of its kind. It's also a great spot for photographs!

Take a trip to Indian Head
Possibly one of the best viewpoints you'll find on Fraser Island, Indian Head is not to be missed. Walk up to the headland for insanely gorgeous views of the coastline at the most easterly point of Fraser Island, at the end of 75 Mile Beach.

See the Champagne Pools
Close by to Indian Head, along 75 Mile Beach, the Champagne Pools are an incredible set of swimming pools you just won't find anywhere else. This must-do spot is the safest place on the island for saltwater swimming, as you're protected in the pools, formed by volcanic rocks, while the waves crash over the rocks. The name Champagne Pools

comes from the tiny bubbles that form, resembling a glass of champagne.

Learn the Dreamtime stories about K'Gari
I don't want to spoil the Dreamtime story for you, but the story of Fraser Island told by the Indigenous Butchella tribe is absolutely beautiful. Hearing it will give you a new found appreciation for the area.

Spot native flora and fauna
As you walk or drive through Fraser Island, switch your senses on high-alert and look out for native flora and fauna. There are some 230 species of bird that call the island home, include peregrine falcons, white-breasted sea eagles, kingfishers, brolgas and the very rare ground parrot. You'll also spot native plants like Banksia, which look like hairy potatoes!

Relax on the beach

Okay, so there are a million things you can do on Fraser Island but it's also really important you slow down, relax and enjoy yourself too. Wake up at sunrise, go down to the beach and have a swim. Just relax, unwind and reconnect. Avoid the hottest/burny parts of the day and make sure you're sun safe!

The End

www.ingramcontent.com/pod-product-compliance
Lightning Source LLC
Chambersburg PA
CBHW031123080526
44587CB00011B/1083